COLLECTION OF CATHOLIC PRAYERS : POWERFUL PRAYERS FOR FAITH AND SPIRITUALITY

AURNY AIRDUVAL

COLLECTION OF CATHOLIC PRAYERS : POWERFUL PRAYERS FOR FAITH AND SPIRITUALITY

Introduction

In a constantly evolving world, prayer remains a source of strength, comfort, and connection to spirituality. Immerse yourself in the very essence of the Catholic faith with our "Collection of Catholic Prayers: Powerful Prayers for Faith and Spirituality." This precious book invites you on an inner journey, where each prayer has been carefully crafted to nourish your soul and strengthen your connection with God.

Whether you seek inspiration, healing, guidance, or gratitude, this collection is filled with prayers deeply rooted in the Catholic tradition, as well as contemporary prayers that address the spiritual needs of today's world. You will find prayers for moments of joy and sorrow, for the challenges of everyday life, and for the deepest aspirations of your heart.

Each prayer is an invitation to immerse yourself in the divine presence, to draw upon the strength of your faith, and to experience the power of Catholic prayer. Whether you are a devout practitioner seeking to deepen your relationship with God or searching for a source of spiritual inspiration, this collection of prayers will accompany you on your faith journey.

Let the sacred words rise from your heart and find resonance within these pages. May each prayer bring you closer to divine grace, bring inner peace, and illuminate the path of spirituality. May these powerful prayers help you strengthen your faith, elevate your spirit, and connect with God's infinite love.

May this "Collection of Catholic Prayers" become your precious companion in the pursuit of peace, joy, and profound spirituality.

Chapter 1

The prayer for healing

Lord, our Healing God,
I turn to you with humility and trust,
Imploring your grace and mercy for my healing.
You know every fiber of my being,
Every affliction and every ailment that troubles me.
Come, Lord, with your healing hand,
Touch my body, mind, and soul,
And restore me to your fullness and vitality.
I pray to you, O God, to dispel all pain,
To heal all wounds and illnesses,
And to restore health and strength in me.
Grant me patience and perseverance during this time
of healing,
As well as confidence in your wisdom and your
purpose for me.
May your love and grace flood my life,
And may I be a living testimony to your healing
power.
I entrust my life into your hands,
And I surrender to your perfect will.
May your healing and peace surround me,
Amen.

This prayer for healing is an invitation to God, as the source of healing, to intervene in our lives to restore our physical, emotional, and spiritual well-being. It expresses our trust in the divine power and compassion, while humbly submitting ourselves to the will of God.

Chapter 2

The prayer for guidance

Lord,
In moments of uncertainty and confusion,
I turn to you to seek your guidance.
I know that you are the way, the truth, and the life,
And that you know the plans you have for me.
Illuminate my path, O God,
Guide me in the decisions I must make.
Grant me the wisdom to discern what is right,
And the courage to follow the path you have laid out
for me.
Open my eyes to see the opportunities before me,
And open my ears to hear your guiding voice.
I entrust my life and aspirations to you,
And I trust you to lead me on the right path.
May your Holy Spirit accompany and counsel me,
And may your light illuminate my steps.
I am grateful for your loving and constant guidance,
And I walk with confidence in the direction you
provide.
In the name of Jesus, my guide and my savior,
Amen.

This prayer for guidance expresses our desire to receive divine direction in our lives. We acknowledge that God is the ultimate guide and that we need His wisdom and discernment to make informed decisions. By entrusting our lives into God's hands, we express our trust in His providence and benevolent guidance.

Chapter 3

The prayer for strength

Lord,
In my weakness and moments of trial,
I turn to you to find strength.
Grant me inner strength to overcome obstacles,
And resilience to persevere in the face of challenges.
When I am discouraged and feel powerless,
Remind me that you are my rock and fortress.
I know that with you by my side, nothing is impossible,
And your power is made perfect in my weakness.
Grant me the strength to resist temptations,
And the steadfastness to remain faithful to your ways.
May your Holy Spirit fill me with your strength,
And may I draw upon your infinite love and grace.
I place my trust in you, O God,
And I know that you will not disappoint me.
In the name of Jesus, my support and my rock,
Amen.

This prayer for strength is an invocation to God to receive the inner strength needed to face life's challenges. It acknowledges our dependence on God and His ability to support and fortify us when we feel weak. In praying for strength, we find the assurance that God is with us, providing the resilience and tenacity required to navigate difficult moments.

Chapter 4

The prayer for gratitude

Lord,
I come before you with a grateful heart,
For all the wonders you have poured into my life.
I am thankful for every breath I take,
For the beauty of the creation that surrounds me,
For the precious relationships that support me,
And for the moments of joy and peace you grant me.
Forgive me for the times I have taken your blessings for granted,
And for the moments when I did not express my gratitude.
Help me cultivate a thankful spirit,
And to see your grace and goodness in every aspect of my life.
May my gratitude be an offering to your infinite love,
And may I share my thankfulness with others.
May I never cease to acknowledge your blessings,
And to praise your name with a heart filled with gratitude.
In the name of Jesus, who is the source of all grace,
Amen.

This prayer of gratitude is a way to thank God for the many blessings He bestows upon us. It reminds us not to take life's gifts for granted and to acknowledge that every good thing comes from God. By expressing our gratitude, we cultivate a positive mindset and an attitude of thankfulness towards God and others.

Chapter 5

The prayer for hope

Lord,
In moments of doubt and despair,
I turn to you to find hope.
Grant me the hope that transcends circumstances,
And lifts me above life's trials.
When I am discouraged and losing confidence,
Remind me that you are the God of hope and restoration.
Help me fix my gaze upon you,
And remember that you are faithful to your promises.
May your Holy Spirit infuse me with your hope,
And may I move forward with confidence on life's path.
When all seems dark and without an exit,
Remind me that you are the light that dispels the darkness.
I place my trust in you, O God,
And believe that you can turn my defeats into victories.
In the name of Jesus, who is our eternal hope,
Amen.

This prayer for hope is an invitation to draw upon trust in God when faced with difficult and uncertain situations. It acknowledges that our hope is not based on current circumstances but on the faithfulness and power of God. In praying for hope, we open ourselves to the possibility of transformation and renewal, relying on the certainty that God is always with us and can lead us to a better future.

Chapter 6

The Prayer for Patience

Lord,
In moments when waiting seems long,
And patience is put to the test,
I turn to you to find patience.
Grant me the grace to remain calm and patient,
And to trust in your perfect timing.
Help me not to worry or be discouraged,
But to believe that you have a plan for me.
Grant me the strength to endure trials,
And the perseverance to continue despite obstacles.
When impatience threatens to take hold of me,
Remind me that patience produces precious fruit.
May your Holy Spirit soothe and guide me,
And may I find peace in you during times of
waiting.
I pray for you to fill my heart with loving patience,
And to help me be patient with others.
In the name of Jesus, who is our example of
patience,
Amen.

This prayer for patience acknowledges that waiting
can be challenging, but it implores God's assistance to

remain calm, perseverant, and patient in life's circumstances. It reminds us that patience is a precious virtue that allows us to grow and mature spiritually. By praying for patience, we open ourselves to the action of the Holy Spirit in our lives, enabling us to navigate moments of waiting with confidence and serenity.

Chapter 7

The prayer for confidence

Lord,
In moments of doubt and uncertainty,
I turn to you to find trust.
Grant me the faith to believe in your constant presence,
And confidence in your infinite wisdom and love.
Help me let go and place my worries in your hands,
Knowing that you care for me and have a plan for my life.
When life's storms threaten to sweep me away,
Remind me that you are my rock and fortress.
May your Holy Spirit fill me with your peace,
And may I find rest in you in times of uncertainty.
I choose to trust your promises,
And to believe that you work all things for my good.
In the midst of life's challenges and trials,
I rely on your faithfulness and find my security in you.
In the name of Jesus, my refuge and shield,
Amen.

This prayer for trust is an invitation to place our faith and trust in God, even when circumstances seem uncertain. It reminds us that God is trustworthy and has a plan for our lives. In praying for trust, we choose to place our worries and fears in God's hands, relying on His wisdom and goodness. This allows us to find the peace and strength needed to move forward with assurance and confidence in our relationship with God.

Chapter 8

The prayer for protection

Lord,
In a world filled with dangers and uncertainties,
I turn to you to seek your protection.
Surround me with your divine presence,
And keep me safe from all harm and danger.
Protect me from the snares of the enemy,
And divert all destructive forces away from me.
May your mighty hand shield me with your protection,
And may your love be my solid fortress.
I ask for your protection for my family, my friends, and all those I love,
May your angel watch over them and keep them safe.
Grant me the wisdom to make prudent decisions,
And to walk the path of righteousness and integrity.
I place my trust in you, O God,
Knowing that you are my refuge and fortress.
In the name of Jesus, who is our protector and defender,
Amen.

This prayer for protection expresses our desire to find a safe refuge in God in a world often dangerous and uncertain. It acknowledges that God is our protector and defender, capable of keeping us safe from harm and danger. In praying for protection, we place our trust in God and submit to His will, knowing that He watches over us with love and kindness. This prayer also reminds us of the importance of seeking divine protection for our loved ones so that they too may be preserved and kept safe.

Chapter 9

The prayer for the family

Lord,
I come before you with a grateful heart,
For the family you have placed in my life.
Bless my family, O God, and protect it,
Grant us the grace to live in harmony and love.
Strengthen our family bonds,
And help us to grow together in faith and understanding.
Give us the wisdom to support each other,
And to be present in moments of joy and sorrow.
Protect us from divisions and discord,
And help us to overcome differences with patience and compassion.
May our home be filled with peace and love,
And may your presence be the foundation of our family.
Bless each member of my family individually,
And meet their spiritual, emotional, and physical needs.
Guide us in your ways, O God,
And may our family be a testimony of your love.
In the name of Jesus, who taught the importance of family love,

Amen.

This prayer for the family is an expression of gratitude to God for the family and a request for blessings and protection for its members. It acknowledges the importance of family bonds and the need for unity and mutual support. In praying for the family, we invite God to intervene in our family lives, strengthen our relationships, and help us grow in love and faith. We also ask God to meet the individual needs of each family member and guide our steps in His ways.

Chapter 10

The prayer for the deceased

O God,
We turn to you in our sorrow and pain,
To pray for those who have left this world and entered into eternal life.
Grant them eternal rest, O Lord,
And let perpetual light shine upon them.
We entrust their souls to you,
Knowing that you are a God full of compassion and mercy.
Console us in our grief and confusion,
And help us find peace in the certainty of your presence.
Allow us to remember them with love and gratitude,
And to continue honoring their memory in our lives.
Give us the strength to live each day with gratitude and generosity,
Recognizing the fragility of life and the value of every moment.
May your grace surround us,
And may we find solace in you and in our faith.
In the name of Jesus, who has conquered death,
Amen.

This prayer for the deceased expresses our desire for peace and eternal rest for those who have left this world. It also acknowledges our need for comfort and support in our grief. In praying for the deceased, we remember their lives with love and gratitude and are reminded of the importance of living each day fully, knowing that our time on earth is limited. We place our trust in God's grace and the promise of eternal life in Jesus Christ.

Chapter 11

The prayer for vocations

O God,
We pray for vocations in your Church,
That men and women may respond to your call with generosity.
Open the hearts and minds of those you are calling,
And grant them the clarity to discern your will.
Give them the courage to say yes to your invitation,
And to embrace the path you have set for them.
Strengthen them in their faith and commitment,
And fill them with your grace for their mission.
Bless them with wisdom and discernment,
So they may guide and serve your people faithfully.
May those who are called find support and encouragement in their journey,
And may the Church always be ready to accompany and train them.
We also pray for those who hesitate or doubt their vocation,
That you may enlighten and guide them on the path meant for them.
In the name of Jesus, who called his disciples to follow him,
Amen.

This prayer for vocations is an invitation to pray for God to call and guide those destined to serve in the Church. It acknowledges that every vocation is a personal call from God and emphasizes the need to listen attentively and respond generously. In praying for vocations, we ask God to inspire and draw individuals who are called to serve in religious, priestly, missionary, or lay ministries. We also pray for discernment in vocations so that those called may discern and follow the path meant for them. We request that the Church be a strong support for those responding to this call, encouraging and training them for their mission.

Chapter 12

The prayer for the sick

Lord,
We turn to you with hearts full of compassion,
To pray for all those who are sick and suffering.
Grant them your healing, O God of mercy,
And alleviate their physical, emotional, and spiritual pain.
Support them in their ordeal,
And give them the strength to face their difficulties.
Surround them with your love and comforting presence,
And allow them to feel your healing touch.
Give them courage and hope,
And help them find comfort in their faith in you.
We also pray for their families and loved ones,
Grant them patience, understanding, and strength to support them.
Guide the hands of doctors, nurses, and caregivers,
And inspire them in their efforts to provide relief and healing.
May your grace abound in the lives of those who are sick,
And may their suffering be transformed into a testimony of faith and resilience.

In the name of Jesus, who healed the sick during his earthly ministry,
Amen.

This prayer for the sick is a request for healing, comfort, and support for those who are suffering. It acknowledges the reality of pain and illness in this world while placing our trust in God as the source of healing and consolation. In praying for the sick, we express our solidarity and compassion for them, while asking God to grant them healing and support in their ordeal. We also pray for the families and loved ones of the sick, that they may be strengthened and encouraged in their supportive role. Finally, we pray for medical wisdom and competence in the treatment of illnesses and that caregivers may be guided in their efforts to provide relief and healing.

Chapter 13

The prayer for wisdom

O God of wisdom,
I turn to you to seek your guidance and discernment.
Grant me the wisdom needed to make right decisions,
And to walk the path of truth and integrity.
Illuminate my mind with your divine light,
And open my eyes to the hidden truth in the situations I encounter.
Give me clarity of thought and insight,
To understand the challenges that come my way and respond with wisdom.
Help me to listen attentively,
And recognize your voice guiding me on the path of life.
May your wisdom permeate my words and actions,
And may I be a channel of your wisdom for others.
Allow me to seize opportunities to learn and grow,
And to cultivate a humility that acknowledges your wisdom is superior to mine.
In the midst of life's uncertainties and complex choices,
I surrender to your wisdom and guidance.
In the name of Jesus, who is wisdom incarnate,

Amen.

This prayer for wisdom expresses our desire to seek divine guidance in our choices and actions. It acknowledges that wisdom comes from God, and we need His enlightenment to make right decisions aligned with His will. In praying for wisdom, we also recognize our humility before God, knowing that His wisdom surpasses our own, and we need to rely on Him to find the path of truth. This prayer invites us to be receptive to God's voice and to cultivate a disposition to learn and grow in our quest for wisdom.

Chapter 14

The Prayer for reconciliation

Lord,
We pray for reconciliation,
That wounded hearts may be healed, and broken relationships may be restored.
Grant us the strength to forgive those who have wronged us,
And to reach out to those we have hurt to seek forgiveness.
Inspire us to extend a hand and build bridges,
Instead of walls, and nourish divisions.
Open our hearts to compassion and empathy,
And help us see the potential for redemption in every person.
Bless those involved in conflicts and divisions,
And grant them the wisdom and courage to seek reconciliation.
Guide our words and actions,
So they may be filled with gentleness, patience, and mutual respect.
May healing and peace spread through our families, communities, and our world,
And may we be instruments of reconciliation in our surroundings.

We entrust all situations of conflict and division to you,
And place our trust in your transformative power.
In the name of Jesus, who reconciled humanity with God through His sacrifice,
Amen.

This prayer for reconciliation is a request for healing, peace, and the restoration of broken relationships. It acknowledges that forgiveness, compassion, and the pursuit of reconciliation are essential elements in overcoming conflicts and divisions. By praying for reconciliation, we open ourselves to the possibility of healing past wounds, restoring broken relationships, and promoting peace in our families, communities, and our world. We ask God to guide us in our words and actions so that they promote reconciliation rather than fuel divisions. Finally, we entrust ourselves to the transformative power of God, knowing that with Him, all things are possible.

Chapter 15

The prayer for justice

O God of justice,
We pray for justice to prevail in our world.
Open our eyes to the injustices that occur,
And inspire us to act with compassion and determination.
Give us the strength to advocate for the rights of the oppressed,
And to work to end exploitation and discrimination.
Support those who are fighting for justice,
And fortify their resolve in the face of adversity.
May those with power and influence act with integrity,
Seeking the common good rather than their own interests.
May laws and systems be just and fair,
And may the innocent be protected and the guilty held accountable.
Help us be champions of justice,
Using our voices, resources, and talents to make a difference.
May the light of truth shine on hidden injustices,
And may justice be restored for those who have been deprived of it.

In the name of Jesus, who preached justice and denounced oppression,
Amen.

This prayer for justice is a request for the rectification of injustices and the establishment of an equitable system. It recognizes that justice is an essential aspect of God's love, and that we are called to act as advocates for justice in our world. By praying for justice, we commit to defending the rights of the oppressed, combating exploitation, and promoting equality for all. We also ask God to fortify those who work for justice and guide those with power and influence to act with integrity. Finally, we pray that truth is revealed and justice prevails, bringing healing and reparation where needed.

Chapter 16

The prayer for children

Lord,
We pray for all the children of the world,
That they may be surrounded by your love and protection.
Bless them with a happy and fulfilling childhood,
Fill their hearts with joy, innocence, and wonder.
Protect them from physical, emotional, and spiritual harm,
And keep them away from anything that might hurt them.
Grant them loving and caring parents,
Who will guide them with wisdom and support their growth.
Support those deprived of their childhood,
Who suffer from violence, neglect, or abandonment.
Provide them with opportunities for education, play, and development,
And help them realize their full potential.
May children be treated with respect and dignity,
And may their fundamental rights be protected by society.
Grant us the wisdom and compassion to support them,

And to create a world where every child can thrive in safety.

In the name of Jesus, who blessed the children and said, 'Let the little children come to me,'

Amen.

This prayer for children is an expression of our love and concern for their well-being. It acknowledges the importance of a happy, protected, and fulfilling childhood for the healthy development of children. In praying for children, we seek protection from the dangers and injustices that threaten them, as well as the blessing of loving and caring relationships with their parents and those around them. We also pray for children who are suffering, deprived of their childhood, or victims of violence, asking for solutions to ensure their safety and well-being. Finally, we commit to being advocates for children's rights and working to create an environment where every child is valued, protected, and supported in their development.

Chapter 17

The prayer for the elderly

Gracious God,
We give thanks for the elderly who enrich our lives.
Bless them with your peace and serenity,
And surround them with your grace and tenderness.
Grant them strength and health for each day,
And bestow moments of joy and happiness upon them.
We thank you for their wisdom and experience,
And for the life lessons they share with us.
Enable them to find meaning and purpose in every stage of their lives,
And help us honor and respect their dignity.
Support them through the challenges of aging,
And encompass them with loving and attentive care.
May society recognize their worth and contributions,
And ensure they are treated with respect and equity.
Grant us the patience and compassion to accompany them,
And to listen to their needs and concerns.
In the name of Jesus, who honored the elderly and said, 'Let the dead bury their dead,' we pray.
Amen.

This prayer for the elderly celebrates their presence and contribution in our lives. It expresses our gratitude for their wisdom, experience, and valuable life lessons they impart to us. In praying for the elderly, we ask God to surround them with peace, health, and moments of joy. We also pray that society recognizes their worth and dignity and ensures they are treated with respect and equity. Finally, we commit to being attentive and loving companions to the elderly, by listening to them, supporting them, and honoring their life journey.

Chapter 18

The prayer for students

O God of all knowledge,
We pray for the students dedicating themselves to their learning.
Grant them clarity of mind and the necessary focus,
So they may absorb knowledge with ease.
Inspire them in their studies and research,
And open their minds to new and stimulating ideas.
Give them perseverance and motivation,
To overcome challenges and obstacles in their path.
Support them in their exams and assessments,
And grant them the serenity to manage stress and anxiety.
Guide them to the right resources and teachers,
Who will help them develop their skills and potential.
Bless their efforts and hard work,
And grant them success in their studies and projects.
May their knowledge be used to serve others,
And may they contribute to making this world a better place.
In the name of Jesus, who grew in wisdom and stature,
Amen.

This prayer for students is a request for wisdom, guidance, and success in their studies. It acknowledges the importance of learning and seeking knowledge in the intellectual and personal development of students. In praying for students, we ask God to inspire, guide, and support them throughout their educational journey. We also pray for them to have the perseverance, motivation, and peace of mind needed to face academic challenges. We ask God to bless them in their efforts and grant them success in their studies and projects. Finally, we pray that the knowledge acquired by students is used to serve others and contributes to the improvement of our world.

Chapter 19

The prayer for religious vocations

O God of all vocations,
We pray for those discerning a call to religious life.
Inspire and guide them in their discernment,
And open their hearts to your call of love and service.
Grant them clarity of mind to recognize your will,
And inner strength to respond generously.
Support them in their doubts and questioning,
And surround them with supportive individuals.
Bestow upon them a deep experience of your love,
And nurture their personal relationship with you.
Grant them the grace of perseverance and commitment,
So they may faithfully live out their religious vocation.
Bless them with the joy and peace that come from you,
And may they be living witnesses of your love in the world.
May your Holy Church be filled with vocations,
And may those who answer your call be supported and guided.

In the name of Jesus, who called his disciples to follow him,
Amen.

This prayer for religious vocations expresses our support and encouragement for those who will discern a call to religious life. It acknowledges the significance of religious vocations in the life of the Church and in bearing witness to God's love in the world. By praying for religious vocations, we implore God to inspire and guide those discerning their calling, to surround them with support, and to help them persevere in their commitment. We pray that they may experience the depth of God's love and live their religious vocation faithfully with joy and peace. We also request that the Church be filled with vocations, and that those who respond to God's call receive support and guidance throughout their journey.

Chapter 20

The Prayer for spouses

O God of love,
We pray for all spouses who have joined their lives in marriage.
Bless them with deep affection and a strong union,
And renew their love for each other every day.
Give them the grace of patience and forgiveness,
That they may overcome difficulties and grow together.
Inspire them in their commitment to each other,
And help them to encourage and support each other on their journey.
Grant them wisdom and understanding,
So that they may care for each other with tenderness.
May their home be a haven of peace and joy,
A place where love and kindness reign supreme.
Protect their marriage from temptation and negative influences,
And strengthen their commitment through life's trials.
Help them to grow together in faith and love for you,

And to bear witness to the love of Jesus in their relationship.
In the name of Jesus, who blessed the marriage at Cana,
Amen.

This prayer for spouses celebrates the sacrament of marriage and seeks divine blessings for married couples. It acknowledges the importance of love, commitment, and mutual understanding within marriage. In praying for spouses, we ask God to bless them with deep affection, a strong union, and a fulfilling relationship. We also pray that they receive support during challenging times, find the ability to forgive, and grow together. We ask God to protect their marriage from negative influences and to strengthen their commitment through life's trials. Finally, we pray that their home may be a place of peace, joy, and love, where their relationship serves as a testimony to the love of Jesus.

Chapter 21

The prayer for singles

O faithful God,

We pray to you for all single people seeking their path in life.

Grant them your guidance and clarity,

That they may discern your will for their future.

Comfort them in times of loneliness and uncertainty,

And comfort their hearts with your love and presence.

Give them inner peace and confidence in you,

So that they can embrace their state in life with serenity.

Help them to find meaning and purpose in their celibacy,

And to live each day fully and joyfully.

Bless them with sincere friendships and rewarding relationships,

Who support and accompany them on their journey.

Allow them to discover and develop their talents and passions,

And use their gifts in your service and for the good of others.

May their celibacy be a period of spiritual growth,

And may they live in confident expectation of your plan for them.

In the name of Jesus, who found his fullness in you, Amen.

This prayer for singles acknowledges their state of life and asks God to guide, comfort, and bless them. It recognizes the challenges and moments of loneliness that singles may face, as well as the opportunities for growth and service available to them. In praying for singles, we ask God to accompany them in their discernment and grant them inner peace and confidence in His will. We also pray that they may live each day to the fullest by developing their talents and dedicating themselves to serving others. Lastly, we request that God bless them with sincere friendships and enriching relationships, helping them live in confident anticipation of His plan for their lives.

Chapter 22

The prayer for those in distress

O compassionate God,
We pray for all those in distress and suffering.
Look with kindness upon those who feel lost, discouraged, or desperate,
And grant them your comfort and loving presence.
Wipe away the tears of those who weep,
And soothe the turmoil of those in anguish.
Strengthen those weakened by life's trials,
And give them the resilience to persevere through adversity.
Grant them hope in the darkest moments,
And let your light shine in the midst of their darkness.
Open doors of relief and support for those in need,
And inspire us to reach out with generosity and compassion.
May your love heal physical, emotional, and spiritual wounds,
And restore peace and joy to their hearts.
We also pray that those in distress find refuge in you,
And that their faith in your power of deliverance and transformation grows.

In the name of Jesus, who promised to be with us in our trials,
Amen.

This prayer for those in distress reminds us of our duty of compassion towards those who suffer. It expresses our request for divine comfort for those who feel lost, discouraged, or desperate. We pray for God to wipe away their tears, soothe their turmoil, and strengthen their courage. We also ask God to open doors of relief and support and inspire us to be instruments of generosity and compassion to those in need. In praying for people in distress, we place our trust in God's healing love, His ability to restore peace and joy, and His presence that accompanies us through life's trials.

Chapter 23

This prayer for the oppressed

O God of justice,
We pray for all those who are oppressed and deprived of their fundamental rights.
Look with compassion on those who suffer injustice, discrimination and exploitation,
And manifest your power to bring them liberation and restoration.
Protect them from abuse of power and violence,
And defend them in their quest for dignity and freedom.
Give them the courage to speak out against injustice and fight for their rights,
And raise up strong voices to plead on their behalf.
Break down the barriers of oppression and discrimination,
And establish a reign of justice and equality over all the earth.
Give us the wisdom and will to engage in the struggle for justice,
And to work for social transformation and the elimination of injustice.
May your presence comfort those who are oppressed,

And may your love strengthen them in their resistance and their quest for dignity.

In the name of Jesus, who proclaimed liberation for the oppressed,

Amen.

This prayer for the oppressed expresses our solidarity with those who are victims of oppression and our call for divine justice. We pray for God to intervene on behalf of the oppressed, protect them from abuses, and free them from all forms of oppression. We ask God to give the oppressed the courage to speak out against injustice and to fight for their rights, and to raise up powerful voices on their behalf. We also pray for social transformation so that the barriers of oppression and discrimination are overturned, and justice and equality prevail. In praying for the oppressed, we recognize the need to engage in the struggle for justice and to work for a world where all human beings are treated with dignity and respect.

Chapter 24

The prayer for leaders

O God of wisdom,
We pray for all the world's leaders, locally, nationally and internationally.
Grant them the wisdom and discernment to make just and informed decisions,
And inspire them to lead with integrity, compassion and respect for human dignity.
Give them the clarity of vision to solve problems and overcome challenges,
And guide them in the pursuit of the common good and justice for all.
Bless them with the strength and courage to face pressures and responsibilities,
And grant them the will to serve with humility and dedication.
Protect them from the temptations of power and selfishness,
And help them to always put the common good before their own personal interests.
Give them the ability to listen with empathy and act with compassion,
And inspire them to work for peace, reconciliation and the well-being of all.

Grant them wise counselors and honest collaborators,
And foster in them a sense of responsibility and accountability.
We also pray that leaders will be open to the voice of your Spirit,
And that they will be guided by your will in all their decisions.
In the name of Jesus, who came as servant of all,
Amen.

This prayer for leaders acknowledges their crucial role in society and asks God to guide them in their responsibilities. It prays that they make informed and just decisions, and lead with integrity and compassion. It requests God's protection from the temptations of power and help in serving with humility and dedication. The prayer also seeks wisdom, discernment, and clarity of vision for leaders to resolve problems and work for the common good. When praying for leaders, it recognizes their need for support, wise advisors, and upright collaborators. It asks God to inspire them to work for peace, reconciliation, and the well-being of all and to listen to the voice of the Spirit in their decisions.

Chapter 25

The prayer for workers

O God, our Creator,
We thank you for the gift of work and the means to provide for our needs.
We pray for all workers, whether employed, self-employed, or unemployed.
Bless their toil and efforts,
And grant them the strength, endurance, and perseverance to fulfill their tasks.
Protect them from physical dangers and occupational risks,
And preserve their physical, mental, and emotional health.
Guide them in their quest for meaning and fulfillment in their work,
And help them find satisfaction and fulfillment in what they do.
Grant them harmonious and respectful working relationships,
And inspire them to collaborate in a spirit of teamwork and solidarity.
Provide them with fair recognition and compensation for their work,

And create job opportunities for those who are unemployed.
We also pray for workers facing injustice, exploitation, and discrimination,
And ask that the dignity and rights of all workers be respected.
In the name of Jesus, who was Himself a worker,
Amen.

This prayer for workers acknowledges the importance of work in our lives and asks God to bless, protect, and guide those who work. We express our gratitude for the gift of work and our appreciation for workers. We pray for their strength, endurance, and perseverance in fulfilling their tasks. We ask God to protect them from physical dangers and preserve their physical, mental, and emotional health. We also pray that they find meaning and fulfillment in their work and enjoy harmonious working relationships. We request that God ensures that all workers are treated with justice, dignity, and respect, and that their rights are protected. In praying for workers, we recognize their value and essential contribution to our society.

Chapter 26

The prayer for conversion

Lord Jesus,

I turn to you with a repentant heart and a sincere desire for change.

I acknowledge my faults, my mistakes, and my poor choices,

And I ask for forgiveness for everything that has drawn me away from you.

I ardently desire a profound conversion of my being,

So that my life may align with your will and teachings.

Grant me the grace of humility to recognize my limitations,

And give me the strength to let go of my sinful attachments and habits.

Come, Holy Spirit, illuminate my inner darkness,

And transform my heart into a place of purity and love.

Guide me on the path of holiness and virtue,

And help me turn to you in prayer, meditation, and the reading of your Word.

Support me in my struggles and temptations,

And give me the grace to resist evil and choose what is good.

Heavenly Father, I entrust my conversion and transformation to you,
And I ask for your constant assistance in growing in faith and holiness.
In the name of Jesus, who came to call sinners to conversion,
Amen.

This prayer for conversion expresses our desire to change internally and draw closer to God. We acknowledge our faults, mistakes, and poor choices, and we ask for forgiveness for everything that has separated us from God. We express our ardent desire for a profound conversion of our being so that our lives align with God's will. We ask the Holy Spirit to enlighten us, transform our hearts, and guide us on the path to holiness. We recognize our constant need for God's grace to resist evil, choose what is good, and grow in faith. By praying for conversion, we open our hearts to divine grace and place our trust in God to help us in our spiritual journey.

Chapter 27

The prayer for humility

Merciful God,
I stand before you with a humble heart, eager to learn humility.

Acknowledge my pride, vanities, and selfish desires,
And help me to surrender them before your greatness and holiness.

Teach me to recognize my dependence on you
And to submit humbly to your will and your plans.

Detach my heart from excessive self-concern,
And open my eyes to the beauty and worth of every person I encounter.

Inspire me to serve others with humility and generosity,
Following the example of Jesus, who became a servant to all.

Grant me the grace to acknowledge my mistakes and seek forgiveness,
And help me grow in compassion and respect for others.

Guide me on the path of humility,
So that I may draw nearer to you and live in accordance with your will.

In the name of Jesus, who is meek and humble of heart,
Amen.

This prayer for humility expresses our desire to cultivate humility in our lives and draw nearer to God with a humble heart. We acknowledge our pride and selfish desires, and we ask God to help us abandon them before His greatness and holiness. We ask God to teach us to recognize our dependence on Him and to submit humbly to His will. We pray that our hearts be detached from excessive self-concern and open to the value of every person. We ask God to inspire us to serve others with humility, following the example of Jesus. We also ask God to guide us on the path of humility so that we may draw nearer to Him and live in accordance with His will. In praying for humility, we recognize our constant need for God's grace to grow in this essential virtue.

Chapter 28

The prayer for redemption

O merciful God,
We turn to you with a deep desire for redemption.
Acknowledge our sins, our mistakes and our weaknesses,
And extend to us your mercy and forgiveness.
We are aware of our inability to save ourselves,
And humbly surrender ourselves to your saving grace.
Through the precious blood of Jesus, shed for our sins,
Purify us and free us from all guilt and the chains of sin.
Give us the strength to resist temptation and choose what is good,
And renew our hearts to do your will.
Help us to forgive those who trespass against us,
as you have forgiven and reconciled us to yourself.
Grant us the grace to live in the freedom of the children of God,
And guide us along the path of holiness and eternal life.
We believe that your mercy is infinite and your love inexhaustible,

And we trust in you for our redemption.
In the name of Jesus, our Redeemer and Saviour,
Amen.

This prayer for redemption expresses our need for God's saving grace and our desire to be liberated from our sins. We acknowledge our inability to save ourselves and humbly surrender to God's mercy and forgiveness. We ask God to purify and free us from all guilt and the chains of sin through the precious blood of Jesus. We seek the strength to resist temptation and choose what is right and the renewal of our hearts according to God's will. We also pray for the grace to forgive those who have wronged us, recognizing that we ourselves have been forgiven and reconciled with God. We ask God to guide us on the path to holiness and eternal life, living in the freedom of God's children. In praying for redemption, we express our faith in God's infinite mercy and love and our trust in Him for our salvation.

Chapter 29

The prayer for protection against evil

Almighty God,
I turn to you with a humble prayer for protection against evil.
I acknowledge the existence of evil in the world and within myself,
And I seek your mighty protection against all forces of evil.
May your love and light dispel the darkness in my life,
And may your truth scatter the lies and illusions of the enemy.
Envelop me with your protective shield,
And strengthen me in my struggle against temptations and harmful influences.
Grant me the wisdom to discern right from wrong,
And the strength to resist the seductions that seek to lead me away from you.
In the name of Jesus, who triumphed over evil through his death and resurrection,
I reject all malevolent authority and power over my life.
May your Holy Spirit guide my steps,

And may your presence be my refuge and fortress at all times.

I place my trust in you, O God,
And I know that you are my faithful protector and defender.

In the midst of trials and spiritual battles,
I know that you are with me, sustaining and preserving me from evil.

May your mighty hand guard and protect me,
And may I walk in the victory and freedom that you offer.

In the name of Jesus, my Savior and Protector,
Amen.

This prayer for protection against evil expresses our desire for divine protection in our lives. We acknowledge the existence of evil in the world and within ourselves, and we ask God to shield us from all the forces of evil. We implore God to envelop our lives with His love and light, to fortify us in our struggle against temptations and harmful influences, and to grant us the wisdom and strength to resist seductions that seek to lead us away from Him. We renounce any malevolent authority and power over our lives in the name of Jesus, who triumphed over evil through His death and resurrection. We place our trust in God as our faithful protector and defender and rely on His presence to be our refuge and fortress at all times. We acknowledge that God is with us amidst trials and spiritual battles, supporting and preserving us from evil. We ask God to keep and protect us and grant us victory and freedom in Him. By praying for protection against evil, we express our confidence in God's power and faithfulness.

Chapter 30

The prayer for patience

Lord, I turn to you with a humble prayer for patience.

I recognise that patience is a virtue that is often difficult for me to practise,

But I believe in your transforming power and compassionate love.

Help me to be patient in times of difficulty and frustration,

When circumstances don't unfold as I expect.

Give me the grace to remain calm and serene in the face of challenges and trials,

And to accept with confidence your perfect plan for my life.

Teach me to wait with joyful expectation and hope,

Knowing that you are in control and that you act in your own good time.

Strengthen me when I'm tempted to impose my own timing,

And help me to submit humbly to your will and purpose.

May patience be a quality that characterises my relationships with others,

Grant me the grace to listen, understand and forgive.

May my patience be a source of peace and inspiration to those around me,
And a manifestation of your love that dwells within me.
Lord, I know that patience is a fruit of the Spirit,
And I ask you to cultivate it in me, day after day.
Grant me the strength and perseverance I need to grow in patience,
And to live in harmony with your divine will.
In the name of Jesus, who showed us the example of patience through his infinite love,
Amen.

This prayer for patience expresses our desire to acquire and cultivate this precious virtue. We acknowledge that patience can be challenging to practice, but we believe in God's transformative power. We ask God to help us be patient in times of difficulty and frustration, confidently accepting His perfect plan for our lives. We also ask God to teach us to wait with joyful and hopeful expectation, knowing that He is in control and acts in His own time. We seek the necessary strength to resist the urge to impose our own timing and to humbly submit to God's will. We pray that patience becomes a quality that characterizes our relationships with others, allowing us to listen, understand, and forgive. We ask God to cultivate patience in us, knowing that it is a fruit of the Spirit. We request the strength and perseverance needed to grow in patience and live in harmony with His divine will. In praying for patience, we acknowledge our dependence on God and seek His grace to develop this virtue in our lives.

Chapter 31

The prayer for prosperity

O beloved God,
I turn to you with a humble prayer for prosperity.
I know that you are the provider of all good things,
and I ask you to bless my life materially and spiritually.
Grant me the wisdom to manage my resources diligently,
And to use my talents and skills fruitfully.
Bless my work and my businesses,
And open doors of opportunity for me.
I ask you to provide for my every need,
And give me the ability to help those in need.
I pray that you will multiply my resources,
And that you make everything I commit to flourish.
But more than material prosperity, I ask you for spiritual prosperity,
May my relationship with you grow stronger every day.
May my life be filled with peace, joy and abundance in you,
And may I be an instrument of your goodness and generosity.
Help me to keep my eyes fixed on you,

And not to be attached to fleeting material riches.

May my prosperity be a testimony to your faithfulness and grace,

And may I share your blessings with others.

In the name of Jesus, who taught us to seek first the kingdom of God,

I pray for prosperity according to your will and for your glory,

Amen.

This prayer for prosperity expresses our desire to be blessed both materially and spiritually by God. We acknowledge that God is the provider of all good things and we ask Him to bless our lives in all aspects. We seek wisdom to manage our resources diligently and to use our talents fruitfully. We ask God to bless our work and endeavors, to open doors of opportunity, and to multiply our resources. However, we recognize that spiritual prosperity is just as important, and we pray for our relationship with God to grow and strengthen each day. We ask God to fill our lives with peace, joy, and abundance in Him and to use us as instruments of His goodness and generosity toward others. We also ask God to help us keep our eyes fixed on Him, not to be attached to fleeting material wealth, and to seek His kingdom first. In praying for prosperity, we acknowledge that all blessings come from God, and we seek to use them wisely and generously, for His glory and for the good of others.

Chapter 32

The prayer for abundance

Beloved God,
I come to you with a prayer for abundance.
I know that you are the provider of all good things,
And I ask you to pour your blessings upon me in abundance.
Grant me the wisdom to recognize and appreciate the wonders of life,
And gratitude for all that you have already provided.
Bless my relationships, my health, and my material resources,
So that I may use them for your honor and to help others.
Open the pathways of abundance in my life,
Creating opportunities, expanding my horizons, and removing obstacles.
Fill my heart with peace and deep joy,
And grant me clarity of mind to make the right decisions.
I pray for your presence in all my endeavors,
And for the success of my efforts.
May my work be fruitful and fulfilling,
And may I find satisfaction and fulfillment in what I do.

I also pray for you to bless my spiritual life,
May my relationship with you deepen and grow in intimacy.
May I be a source of blessing to others,
Sharing your gifts and extending your grace.
In the name of Jesus, who came that we may have life in abundance,
I pray for abundance according to your will and for your glory,
Amen.

This prayer for abundance expresses our desire to be filled and blessed in all aspects of our lives. We acknowledge that God is the provider of all good things and we ask Him to pour His blessings upon us in abundance. We seek wisdom to appreciate the wonders of life and gratitude for all that God has already provided. We pray for God to bless our relationships, our health, and our material resources so that we can use them for His glory and to help others. We ask God to open the pathways of abundance in our lives by creating opportunities, expanding our horizons, and removing obstacles. We pray for our hearts to be filled with peace and deep joy and for the clarity of mind necessary to make the right decisions. We request God's blessing on our work, making it fruitful and fulfilling, and granting us satisfaction and fulfillment. We also pray for God to bless our spiritual lives, for our relationship with Him to deepen and grow in intimacy. We ask God to make us sources of blessing to others by sharing His gifts and extending His grace. In praying for abundance, we acknowledge that all good things come from God and seek to receive them with gratitude, use them responsibly, and share them generously with others.

Chapter 33

The prayer for love of neighbour

O Merciful God,
I turn to you with a prayer for loving our neighbours.
Give me a heart filled with compassion,
To see and understand the needs of others.
Help me set aside my own interests,
And reach out to those in need.
Grant me the strength to forgive those who have hurt me,
And to offer reconciliation and peace.
Inspire me to care for the sick, the afflicted, and the oppressed,
And be a source of comfort and hope to them.
May I be attentive to loneliness and hidden sufferings,
And bear witness to your love through tangible actions.
Help me practice mutual support and solidarity,
By sharing my resources and aiding those in need.
May I not judge others, but treat them with kindness,
Acknowledging that we are all your beloved children.
Guide me in performing good deeds,

And may my actions reflect your grace and mercy.

In the name of Jesus, who taught us to love our neighbour as ourselves,

I pray for a love of neighbour according to your will and for your glory,

Amen.

This prayer for love of neighbour expresses our desire to love and serve our fellow human beings with compassion and generosity. We ask God to give us a heart filled with compassion to see and understand the needs of others. We seek the strength to forgive those who have hurt us and offer reconciliation and peace. We ask God to inspire us to care for the sick, the afflicted, and the oppressed, and be a source of comfort and hope to them. We commit to being attentive to loneliness and hidden suffering, and to bear witness to God's love through tangible actions. We request God's help in practicing mutual support and solidarity by sharing our resources and aiding those in need. We pledge not to judge others but to treat them with kindness, acknowledging that we are all beloved children of God. We ask God to guide us in performing good deeds so that our actions reflect His grace and mercy. In praying for love of neighbour, we recognize that love is the foundation of our relationship with God and with others, and we seek to manifest this love in our words and actions.

Chapter 34

The prayer for the communion of saints

O eternal God,
I turn to you with a prayer for the communion of saints.
I give thanks for the bond that unites us as believers,
Beyond the boundaries of space and time.
We are all members of one great spiritual family,
united by faith in your beloved Son, Jesus Christ.
I pray for our brothers and sisters in the faith who have gone before us,
For those who have died and rest in you.
Grant them eternal rest and endless joy,
And let your light shine on them forever.
I also pray for those who are still on this earth,
For all those who seek the truth and struggle in their faith.
Strengthen us in your love and in our commitment to you,
And may our witness inspire others.
Help us to share your gifts and grace,
And to be instruments of peace and reconciliation.
May we be united in prayer and worship,
And may our love for one another reflect your perfect love.

In the name of Jesus, our Lord and Brother,
I pray for the communion of saints according to your will and for your glory,
Amen.

This prayer for the communion of saints contained in this book expresses our gratitude for the bond that unites us as believers, transcending the boundaries of space and time. We give thanks for our vast spiritual family, united by faith in Jesus Christ. We pray for our brothers and sisters in the faith who have gone before us, asking God to grant them eternal rest and endless joy. We also pray for those still on this earth, that they may be strengthened in their faith and that their testimony may be a source of inspiration. We ask God to help us share His gifts and grace, and to be instruments of peace and reconciliation. We desire to be united in prayer and worship, and for our love for one another to reflect God's perfect love. In praying for the communion of saints, we acknowledge our unity in Christ and our interdependence within the great family of God.

Chapter 35

The prayer for sanctification

O Holy God,
I come to you with a prayer for sanctification.
Purify my heart and thoughts,
And help me live a life in accordance with your will.
Teach me to turn away from sin,
And choose the path of righteousness and holiness.
Fill me with your Holy Spirit,
So that I may be transformed into your image each day.
Grant me wisdom to understand your Word,
And the strength to put it into practice in my life.
Assist me in persevering in prayer and meditation,
And seeking your presence with fervor and constancy.
May my life be a living testimony of your love and truth,
And may I positively influence those around me.
Guide me in my relationships and actions,
So that everything I do is for your glory.
Give me a burning heart for you,
And a will surrendered to your direction.
May I be an instrument of your grace and mercy,
To spread your love and light in the world.

In the name of Jesus, who is holy and worthy of all worship,

I pray for sanctification according to your will and for your glory,

Amen.

This prayer for sanctification expresses our desire to grow in holiness and dedicate ourselves entirely to God. We ask God to purify our hearts and thoughts and help us live a life in accordance with His will. We seek His grace to turn away from sin and choose the path of righteousness and holiness. We ask God to fill our being with His Holy Spirit so that we may be transformed into His image each day. We desire to understand His Word and put it into practice, seeking His presence in prayer and meditation. We wish for our lives to be a living testimony of His love and truth, positively influencing those around us. We request God's guidance in our relationships and actions, so that everything we do is for His glory. We seek a burning heart for God and a will surrendered to His direction. We desire to be instruments of His grace and mercy, spreading His love and light in the world. By praying for sanctification, we acknowledge our constant need for God's grace to grow in holiness and become more like Him.

Chapter 36

The Prayer for unity

O God of love,
I turn to you with a prayer for unity.
We live in a divided and fragmented world,
But we believe in your power to bring all believers together.
Help us overcome our differences and prejudices,
And to see one another as brothers and sisters in Christ.
Grant us a spirit of humility and compassion,
So that we may reach out and listen to one another.
Heal the wounds of the past and dispel misunderstandings,
So that love and truth may prevail in our relationships.
Inspire us to work together for your Kingdom,
In mutual respect and harmony.
May our unity be a powerful testimony of your love,
And draw those who are lost and divided to you.
Bless all those who labor for unity in your Church,
And grant them wisdom, strength, and perseverance.
In the name of Jesus, who prayed that all believers may be one,

I pray for unity according to your will and for your glory,
Amen.

This prayer for unity expresses our desire to see all believers united in love and truth. We acknowledge the divisions present in the world, but we believe in God's power to bring all believers together. We ask God to help us overcome our differences and prejudices, and to see one another as brothers and sisters in Christ. We seek a spirit of humility and compassion to reach out and listen to each other. We request God to heal the wounds of the past and dispel misunderstandings so that love and truth may prevail in our relationships. We are inspired to work together for the Kingdom of God in mutual respect and harmony. We desire our unity to be a powerful testimony of God's love, drawing those who are lost and divided to Him. We bless all those who labor for unity in the Church, asking for the wisdom, strength, and perseverance needed. In praying for unity, we express our desire to see the Church united, reflecting God's love and truth in the world.

Chapter 37

The prayer for understanding

O God of all wisdom,
I turn to you with a prayer for understanding.
Teach me to grasp the mysteries of life,
And discern the hidden spiritual truths.
Grant me clarity of thought and the illumination of your Spirit,
So that I may comprehend the depth of your Word and your will.
Open the eyes of my heart to see beyond appearances,
And recognize your presence and action in my life.
Bestow upon me the wisdom to ask the right questions,
And the patience to await your answers in confidence.
Help me cultivate an open and receptive mindset,
So that I may learn from others and grow in understanding.
Guide me on the path of knowledge and truth,
Illuminating my mind with the light of your love and wisdom.
Inspire me to seek truth with passion and perseverance,

And always remain humble in my quest for understanding.

May my understanding be marked by compassion and grace,

And may it serve to glorify your name and bless those around me.

In the name of Jesus, who is Wisdom incarnate,

I pray for understanding according to your will and for your glory,

Amen.

This prayer for understanding expresses our desire to receive wisdom and illumination from God to comprehend the mysteries of life and spiritual truths. We ask God to teach us to understand the mysteries of life and discern hidden spiritual truths. We seek clarity of thought and the illumination of God's Spirit to grasp the depth of His Word and His will. We desire God to open the eyes of our hearts to see beyond appearances and recognize His presence and action in our lives. We ask God to grant us the wisdom to ask the right questions and the patience to await His answers in confidence. We wish to cultivate an open and receptive mindset, learning from others and growing in our understanding. We ask God to guide us on the path of knowledge and truth, illuminating our minds with the light of His love and wisdom. We are inspired to seek truth with passion and perseverance, remaining humble in our quest for understanding. We desire our understanding to be marked by compassion and grace, serving to glorify God and bless those around us. In praying for understanding, we acknowledge our need for God's wisdom and illumination to grasp the profound truths of life and grow in our relationship with Him.

Chapter 38

The prayer for compassion

O God full of compassion,
I turn to you with a prayer for compassion.
Fill my heart with your compassionate love,
And open my eyes to see the suffering around me.
Give me a heart sensitive to the needs of others,
And inspire me to act with kindness and generosity.
Help me to listen attentively to the stories of others,
And to welcome them with empathy and
understanding.
May I not judge, but reach out with compassion,
To offer true comfort, assistance, and healing.
May my compassion extend to the marginalized and
the excluded,
To the oppressed, the sick, and those in need.
Inspire me to be an instrument of your love in the
world,
To spread compassion and bring healing.
May my life reflect your grace and mercy,
And may my actions testify to your unconditional
love.
In the name of Jesus, who was the embodiment of
compassion,

I pray for compassion according to your will and for your glory,
Amen.

This prayer for compassion expresses our desire to be filled with the compassion of God and to be instruments of His love in the world. We ask God to fill our hearts with His compassionate love and to open our eyes to see the suffering around us. We seek a heart sensitive to the needs of others and an inspiration to act with kindness and generosity. We ask God to help us listen attentively to the stories of others and to welcome them with empathy and understanding. We wish not to judge but rather to reach out with compassion to offer true comfort, assistance, and healing. We desire our compassion to extend to the marginalized, the excluded, the oppressed, the sick, and those in need. We are inspired to be instruments of God's love in the world, spreading compassion and bringing healing. We hope that our lives reflect God's grace and mercy, and that our actions testify to His unconditional love. In praying for compassion, we acknowledge our dependence on God to receive and share His compassionate love.

Chapter 39

The prayer for purification

O Holy and Purifying God,
I turn to you with a prayer for purification.
Look deep into my heart,
And cleanse me from all my faults and past
mistakes.
Wash away my impure thoughts,
And free me from the bonds of selfishness and
pride.
Create in me a pure and sincere heart,
Filled with love, kindness and compassion.
Remove from my life everything that distances me
from you,
And guide me along the path of holiness and truth.
Give me the strength to resist temptation,
And the wisdom to choose good over evil.
Forgive me for my past mistakes,
And help me to grow in your grace and love.
May your Holy Spirit burn in me like a purifying
fire,
consuming all that is impure and leading me to
holiness.
In the name of Jesus, who shed His blood for our
purification,

I pray for cleansing according to your will and for your glory,
Amen.

This prayer for purification expresses our desire to be cleansed from our faults, impure thoughts, and negative actions, in order to draw closer to the holiness of God. We ask God to look into the depths of our hearts and purify us from all our faults and past mistakes. We wish to be washed from impure thoughts and freed from the bonds of selfishness and pride. We desire God to create in us a pure and sincere heart, filled with love, kindness, and compassion. We seek the removal of anything that draws us away from God and guidance on the path of holiness and truth. We ask God to give us the strength to resist temptations and the wisdom to choose good over evil. We seek forgiveness for our past mistakes and help to grow in the grace and love of God. We wish for the Holy Spirit of God to burn in us like a purifying fire, consuming all that is impure and leading us to holiness. In praying for purification, we acknowledge our need for God's purifying action in our lives and our desire to draw closer to His holiness.

Chapter 40

The prayer for perseverance

O God of all perseverance,
I turn to you with a prayer for perseverance.
In moments of discouragement and doubt,
Give me the strength to stand firm in my faith.
When trials and difficulties arise,
Grant me the courage to persevere and not give up.
Help me keep my eyes fixed on you,
And to find my strength and hope in you alone.
May your Word be a lamp on my path,
Illuminating and guiding me in dark times.
Give me confidence in your providence,
Knowing that you are always with me, supporting
and strengthening me.
Grant me the patience to wait for your promises,
And the perseverance to continue praying and
seeking your will.
In the midst of obstacles and failures,
Remind me that you are the God of second chances
and restoration.
May my perseverance testify to my faith in you,
And glorify your name in my life.
In the name of Jesus, who persevered to the cross,

I pray for perseverance according to your will and for your glory,
Amen.

This prayer for perseverance expresses our desire to remain firm and steadfast in our faith, despite difficulties and obstacles. We ask God to give us the strength to stand firm in our faith, even when we are discouraged or plagued by doubt. We seek the courage to persevere and not give up when trials and difficulties arise. We ask God to help us keep our eyes fixed on Him, to find our strength and hope in Him alone. We desire for His Word to be a lamp on our path, illuminating and guiding us in dark times. We request confidence in God's providence, knowing that He is always with us, supporting and strengthening us. We ask for patience to wait for His promises and perseverance to continue praying and seeking His will. We ask God to remind us that He is the God of second chances and restoration, even in the midst of obstacles and failures. We hope that our perseverance testifies to our faith in God and glorifies His name in our lives. In praying for perseverance, we acknowledge our dependence on God and our need for His strength and support to persevere in our walk with Him.

Chapter 41

The prayer for hope

O God of all hope,
I turn to you with a prayer for hope.
In times of despair and sadness,
Give me the strength to believe in a better future.
When the obstacles seem insurmountable,
Remind me that you are greater than all my problems.
Help me to keep my eyes fixed on you,
And find comfort in your constant presence.
Let your Spirit blow over me like a wind of hope,
Renewing my faith and rekindling my trust in you.
Give me the ability to see beyond my present circumstances,
And to believe in your promises that cannot be shaken.
Grant me the inner peace that comes from hope in you,
And the certainty that you are with me every step of the way.
In the midst of darkness, light a beacon of hope,
Lighting my path and guiding my steps towards your infinite love.

May my hope in you be a vibrant testimony to your grace,
And a source of encouragement to those in need.
In the name of Jesus, who is our eternal hope,
I pray for hope according to your will and for your glory,
Amen.

This prayer for hope expresses our desire to find strength and comfort in hope in God, even in the most challenging moments. We ask God to give us the strength to believe in a better future, even when overwhelmed by despair and sadness. We seek His constant presence and comfort to help us keep our eyes fixed on Him. We wish for His Spirit to blow upon us like a wind of hope, renewing our faith and reviving our confidence in Him. We ask God to grant us the ability to see beyond present circumstances and to believe in His unshakable promises. We request inner peace that comes from hope in God and the certainty of His presence at every step of our journey. We desire our hope in God to be a vibrant testimony of His grace and a source of encouragement for those in need. In praying for hope, we turn to God as our ultimate source of hope and comfort, recognizing that our hope is rooted in Him.

Chapter 42

The prayer for transformation

O God of transformation,
I turn to you with a prayer for transformation.
In my weakness and imperfections,
I seek your grace to change me.
Penetrate the depths of my being,
And work within me to make me more like you.
Break the chains that bind me,
And free me from the habits and sins that hold me back.
Let your light shine in the shadows of my life,
And transform my thoughts, words and actions.
Open my eyes to your truth,
And help me to walk in your ways of justice and love.
Give me a gentle and compassionate heart,
That reflects your grace to others.
Turn my fear into courage
And my sadness into joy in your presence.
Renew my mind and soul,
And guide me on the path of spiritual growth.
Let your transformation in me be a living testimony,
Of your power and grace at work in my life.

In the name of Jesus, who gave his life for my transformation,
I pray for transformation according to your will and for your glory,
Amen.

This prayer for transformation expresses our desire to see our lives transformed by the grace of God. We acknowledge our weakness and imperfections, and we seek God's grace that can change us from within. We invite God to penetrate the depths of our being and work in us to make us more like Him. We ask God to break the chains that bind us and free us from habits and sins that hold us back. We desire His light to illuminate the areas of darkness in our lives and transform our thoughts, words, and actions. We request God to open our eyes to His truth and help us walk in His paths of justice and love. We seek a gentle and compassionate heart that reflects His grace towards others. We hope that our fear turns into courage and our sorrow into joy in His presence. We ask God to renew our mind and soul and guide us on the path of spiritual growth. We desire that the transformation worked in us is a living testimony to the power and grace of God. In praying for transformation, we surrender to God's work in our lives, recognizing that He is the one working in us to transform us according to His will and for His glory.

Chapter 43

The prayer for wonder

O marvellous God,
I turn to you with a prayer of wonder.
Open my eyes to see the beauty of your creation,
The majestic mountains, the vast oceans, the twinkling stars.
Awaken in me a heart that marvels at your greatness,
The complexity of nature, the delicate details of a flower, the song of the birds.
Help me to see your presence in the simple things of life,
In a ray of sunshine that lights up a room, in a breeze that caresses my face.
Inspire me to recognise your daily gifts,
The food on my table, the warmth of a home, precious relationships.
Let my spirit be filled with gratitude and admiration,
For the richness of your creation and for your infinite love.
May every moment be an occasion for praise and wonder,
As I contemplate your work and acknowledge your presence within me.

In the name of Jesus, who revealed your eternal love to us,

I pray for wonder according to your will and for your glory,

Amen.

This prayer for wonder expresses our desire to see the beauty of creation and to recognize the greatness of God in all things. We ask God to open our eyes to the magnificence of His creation—from majestic mountains to vast oceans to twinkling stars. We seek a heart that marvels at His greatness, the complexity of nature, and the delicate details of each element of His creation. We ask God to help us perceive His presence in the simple things of life—in sunbeams that brighten our days and breezes that gently touch our faces. We wish to be inspired to recognize and appreciate the daily gifts God grants us, whether it's the food on our tables, the warmth of a home, or precious relationships. We hope our minds will be filled with gratitude and admiration, with every moment becoming an opportunity for praise and wonder at God's work. We pray for our capacity to marvel to grow and for us to recognize God's presence within and around us. In praying for wonder, we turn to God as the ultimate source of all beauty and wonder, offering Him our praise and gratitude.

Chapter 44

The prayer for praise

O wonderful God,
I turn to you with a prayer of praise.
I raise my voice to proclaim your greatness,
your infinite power, your unfathomable wisdom.
You are the Creator of the universe,
the breath of life in all things.
I praise you for your goodness and your generosity,
For your grace that embraces every day.
You are faithful and constant in your love,
Your mercy is renewed every morning.
I praise you for your presence that surrounds me,
For your Spirit who guides and comforts me.
Let all creation praise you,
The heavens and the earth sing your glory.
May my life be an offering of praise,
A living testimony to your infinite love.
May my words and actions magnify you,
May my heart be filled with gratitude and joy.
In the name of Jesus, who is worthy of all praise,
I pray for praise according to your will and for your glory,
Amen.

This prayer for praise expresses our desire to praise and worship God for His greatness, goodness, and faithfulness. We proclaim the greatness of God, His infinite power, and unfathomable wisdom. We praise Him as the Creator of the universe and as the breath of life in all things. We express gratitude for His kindness, generosity, and grace that accompany us each day. We acknowledge His faithfulness and constant love, as well as His mercy that is renewed every morning. We praise Him for His surrounding presence, for the Holy Spirit that guides and comforts us. We desire that all of creation may praise Him, that the heavens and the earth may sing His glory. We offer our lives as an offering of praise, a living testimony of His infinite love. We wish that our words and actions magnify God, and that our hearts are filled with gratitude and joy. In praying for praise, we turn to God with gratitude and adoration, recognizing His worth and supremacy, and offering Him our praise and worship.

Table of contents

Printed in Great Britain
by Amazon

45647363R00061